MEDIA FOCUS

Television

Paul Illidge

Copp Clark Pitman Ltd.
A Longman Company
Toronto

ISBN 0-7730-4974-6

CANADIAN CATALOGUING IN PUBLICATION DATA

Illidge, Paul
Television

(Media focus)
ISBN 0-7730-4974-6

1. Television — Canada. 2. Television — United States. 3. Television — Canada Problems, exercises, etc. 4. Television — United States — Problems, exercises, etc. I. Title. II. Series.

PN1992.3.C3I55 1991 791.45′0971 C91-093340-5

Editing: *June Trusty*
Photo Research: *Melanie Sherwood*
Cover and Text Design: *Holly Fisher & Associates*
Cover Illustration: *Valerie Sinclair*
Typesetting: *Compeer Typographic Services Ltd.*
Printing and Binding: *T.H. Best Company, Ltd.*

Copp Clark Pitman Ltd.
2775 Matheson Blvd. East
Mississauga, Ont.
L4W 4P7

Written, printed, and bound in Canada

INTRODUCTION

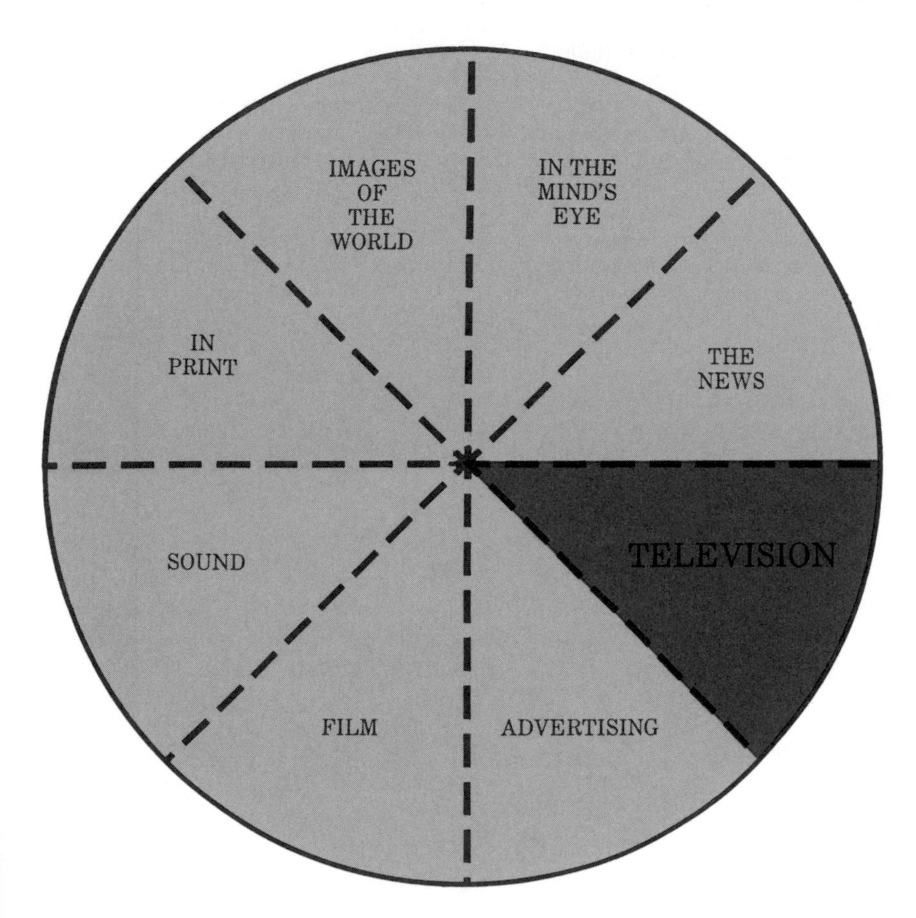

The mass media are the various means we use to communicate ideas and information to large audiences throughout the world. Today, almost any event occurring anywhere in the world can become common knowledge at the touch of a button or the turn of a page. Thus, the mass media have helped turn our world into a "global village."

With so much information from various media bombarding us, we need a means to analyse and organize it so that we can deal with it.

Media Focus will help you acquire an understanding of the various media and how they affect you every day.

Stills from: The Young and the Restless courtesy Columbia Pictures Television; Jeopardy, The Wonder Years, Roseanne, Doogie Howser, M. D., Growing Pains, 20/20 courtesy ABC; The Cosby Show, Heat of the Night, Bonanza, The David Letterman Show, Miami Vice courtesy NBC; The Mary Tyler Moore Show courtesy CBS; Profiles of Nature, Science of Architecture, Télé-français, 17, rue Laurier, C'est Chouette, The Elephant Show, Polka Dot Door courtesy TV Ontario; Sportsline courtesy Global TV; Mr. Dressup, The National, Degrassi High, Market Place, Street Cents, Gemini Awards, Nature, The Don Messer Show, Front Page Challenge, The Plouffe Family, The Beachcombers, Street Legal courtesy CBC; Back to the Future III courtesy The Metropolitan Museum of Modern Art (Film Stills), New York; Live It Up, The Campbells courtesy CTV; Twin Peaks courtesy Lynch-Frost Productions.
Page 21 Courtesy Club Med.
Page 22 courtesy Coca-Cola Company of Canada.
Pages 37, 74 Canapress Photo Service.
Pages 45, 51, 53 courtesy Peter Koritar.
Page 79 Courtesy Northern Service Television.
The publisher gratefully acknowledges the assistance of Bill Elliott and June McCulla of Global Television in producing this module.

CONTENTS

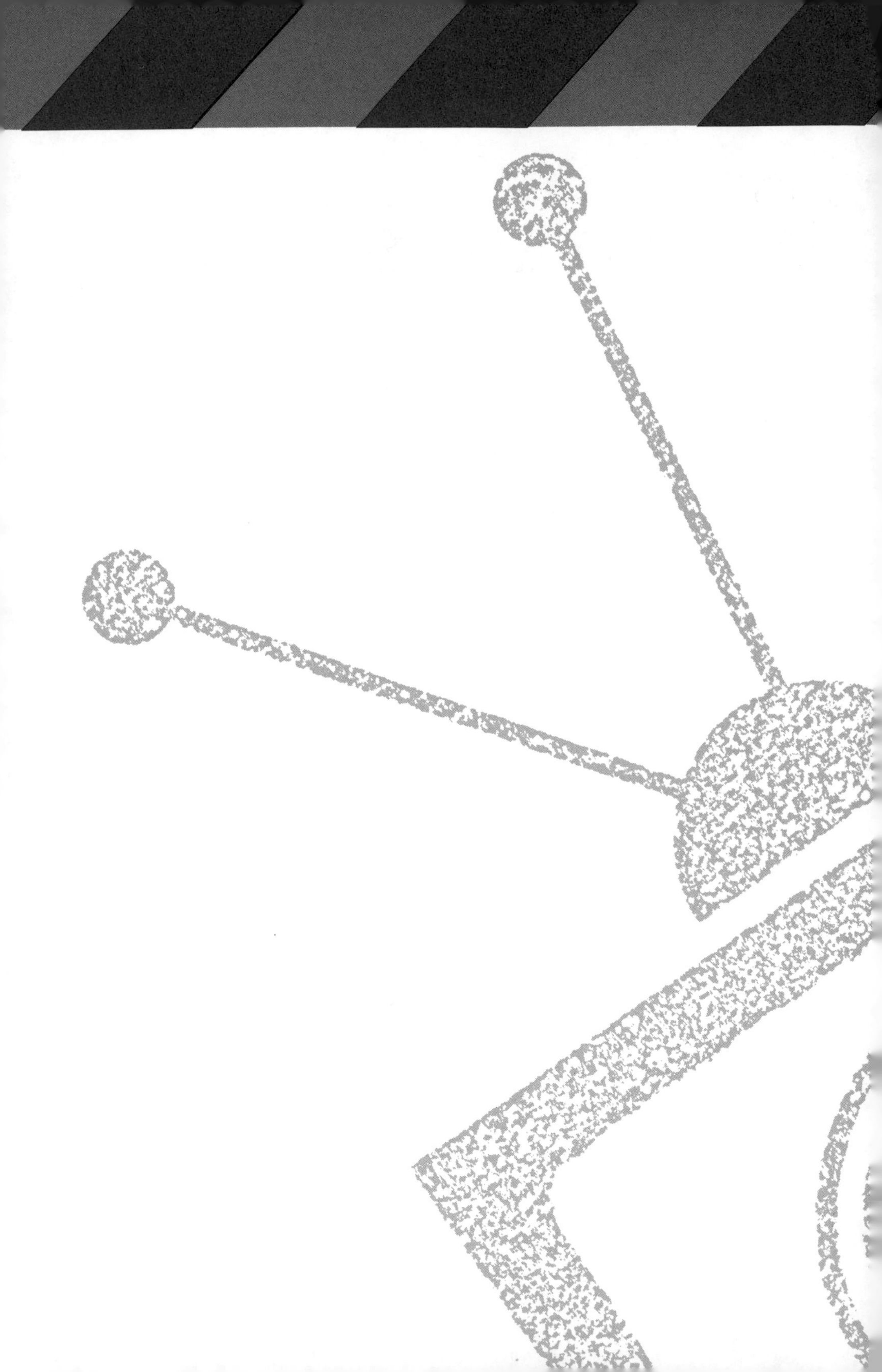

MEDIA FOCUS

1

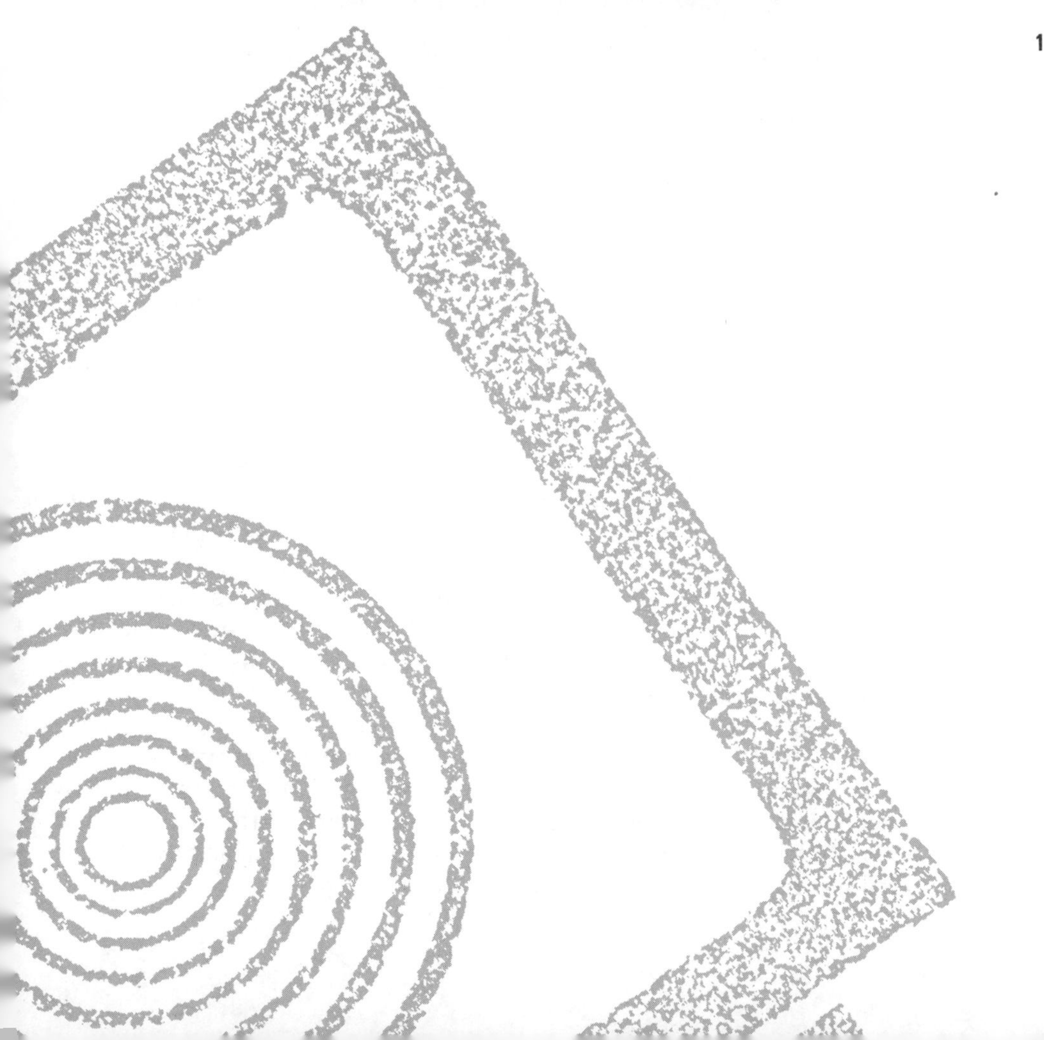

THE WORLD IS WATCHING

Do you watch television? Why or why not? What types of programs do you enjoy? Do you watch programs such as those shown in the photographs? Do these programs depict real-life experiences or imaginary ones? Does it matter which they depict? What types of things do you find out by watching television? How does television affect the way you look at the world?

Those are a lot of questions to consider, but they need to be asked, both of ourselves and others. Television is such an everyday, accepted part of our lives, that we aren't always able to appreciate its value or its effect on us until we have answers that perhaps give us some perspective.

The shows pictured here represent a small sampling of the variety from which television viewers can choose. Amusement, education, intrigue, news, sports, cultural enrichment, shock, violence, and horror are all available in full colour at the push of a button.

Every one of the world's 148 countries has television. Since so many people, in so many places, can see something on television at exactly the same time, TV is considered to be one of the **mass media**. News, weather, sports, history, and lifestyles from around the globe are at our fingertips on the nearly 1 billion television sets in the world.

Anyone born in Canada after 1952 grew up with television. Before then, people depended on the other mass media — radio, books, newspapers, magazines, and movies—for news, education, and entertainment. With the advent of television, suddenly people could sit in their own living rooms and watch events as they occurred, knowing that, in many other parts of the world, other people were watching exactly the same thing.

THE
NATIONAL

The late Marshall McLuhan, a famous Canadian who studied the various forms of communication, once said that television was powerful enough to cause personal changes in how people looked at the world around them. He believed that, even if people did not realize it, TV influenced most aspects of their lives, from the way they dressed, ate, and smelled, to the way they felt about family, friends, school, and the world.

Many people feel that television has made the world smaller, that it has made people all over the world feel closer to people in other countries because they know more about these people and have actually seen them living their everyday lives. Some people point to television as a great educator, making available vast amounts of information in an easy-to-absorb way. Television has also been identified as a valuable provider of:

- Up-to-date news (broadcast as

"Degrassi High" is a Canadian program that was highly popular with viewers during the late 1980s.

it happens anywhere in the world).
- Entertainment (comedy, drama, suspense, mystery, music).
- Cultural enrichment (making available music, plays, opera, ballet, etc., that people might otherwise not be able to afford to see).
- Inspiration (religious programs).
- Companionship (providing a window on the world for lonely or housebound people).
- Babysitting services (many children will sit quietly in front of a TV for long periods of time, freeing their parents for household tasks or other home activities).

Other people say that television has many negative effects. They feel that television makes it too easy for people to obtain information and that it feeds people pre-formed opinions that affect their ability to think for themselves. These critics contend that

A top-rated show with adolescents in 1989, "The Wonder Years" depicts a 14-year-old's life in the 1960s, with a voice-over commentary by the teenager as an adult.

few people now read material that requires the use of imagination. Another criticism is that television interferes with people's personal communication with each other because TV-watching has replaced conversation and other family activities. And a growing complaint is that television emphasizes, and therefore encourages, violence and lawbreaking.

Despite these varying opinions, statistics show that television plays a large part in many people's lives. For example, a major program aired in Canada during peak viewing times can attract more than 2.5 million people, as compared with approximately:

- 200 000 radio listeners of large urban stations during peak hours.
- 500 000 readers per day of Canada's largest daily newspaper.
- One million readers per month of Canada's larger consumer magazines.

Television is the most massive of the mass media, here and around the world. ■

"Doogie Howser, M.D.," and "Growing Pains" were two favourite family shows in the late 1980s.

F·Y·I

Of the 9.5 million households in Canada, 98% have one or more television sets, 93% of which are colour sets. Canadians watch an estimated 24 hours of TV each week. This means that Canadians watch a total of more than 30 billion hours of television each year, the equivalent of 75 000 years!

Switching Channels

1. Look back at the reasons given on page 11 for watching television. Add any other reasons you can think of.
2. Estimate how much of your time is spent watching TV, compared with time spent doing other things such as attending school, reading, playing sports, listening to music, working at a part-time job, doing chores, or sleeping. Compare your results with those of others in the class.
3. List your four favourite TV programs. Imagine that you live in a South American jungle and have never had contact with the outside world. Someone shows you your favourite programs. What would be your impression of the outside world, based on these programs?
4. If you could appear on TV, what kind of program would you want to appear on? Why?

Countdown to Air

1. For a period of one week, compile a log of all of the TV programs that you watch. Develop a format that everyone can use. Then, for each program, record the information listed below. Save this log for an upcoming activity.

   Time of day program watched
   Name of program
   Type of program
   Reason for watching
   What you did while you watched

   General comments:
   Was it worthwhile, a waste of time, or something in between?
   Would you watch the program again?
   Would you recommend it to others?

2. As a class, compile the individual student TV logs into a class log. For each time period, list the programs according to how many people watched a particular program. For example, if most students watched a particular program at a particular time, the name of that program should appear first. In case of a tie, list the programs alphabetically and put an asterisk after the program

names to indicate a tie. What types of programs are preferred by the majority of your classmates? Save this log for later use.

3. Reread Marshall McLuhan's comment about television's effect on people. How do you feel about it? Is the effect of TV on people positive or negative? Discuss with your classmates.
4. Discuss in a small group one or more of the three following items.

   a) Find out which current programs deal with high school life. Watch several episodes. In your opinion, do any of these programs present a realistic picture of high school life? Can you identify classmates who resemble some of the characters? When issues such as drug use and alcoholism are featured, how are they handled? Do they relate to real life?

   b) If "The Wonder Years" represents family life in the 1960s realistically, how did family life then differ from family life now, or how was it similar? Talk to someone who experienced family life in the 1960s to find out how true-to-life "The Wonder Years" is.

   c) Choose two programs that are about families. (The TV families might not be typical ones, but you should be prepared to say why you consider the characters a family.) What similarities are there between them in depicting family life? What differences? Are they true to life? What point of view do they express about family life? What characteristics make a successful television "family"? Would any family you know make a successful TV family?

On the Set

Choose a location in your community (perhaps a busy street in a business district or a shopping mall) and, on a map, divide it into four areas. Then divide your class into four groups and assign an area to each group. Equipped with cassette tape recorders and a video camera, go to the assigned area, stop passersby, and ask them if they would assist you in a survey that your class is conducting. Then ask them questions similar to the following or ones that you have originated. **Note:** If you choose a shopping mall, you might have to obtain permission from the mall's management to carry out your survey.

1. How many hours of television do you estimate that you watch in an average day?
2. Are you watching more or less TV recently? (If there's been a change in viewing habits, ask why.)
3. What is the longest period of time that you have ever gone without watching TV? (If the

time period named is a rather long one, ask why.)
4. When did you first see television? What are your earliest memories of it?
5. What was the last TV program that you watched?
6. What did you like or dislike about the program?
7. What type of TV programs would you like to see more of?
8. What does TV mean to you? Why?

After each interview, record in your notebook the gender, approximate age of each subject (under 10 years of age; 10–20; 20–30; middle-aged; older) and any information that the subject volunteers, such as occupation.

Once you have collected the necessary information, prepare a profile of the modern TV viewer. How many males did you interview? How many females? How many subjects were in each age group? Did a subject's gender or age group seem to affect the amount of TV they watch or the programs chosen? Be sure to include in your report the questions you asked and the total number of people in your survey. Compare and contrast your findings with your personal and class profiles. Save your videotapes for a later project. ■

THE NUMBERS GAME

You are an advertiser wanting to obtain maximum exposure for the product you are selling. Should you advertise on TV or use some other medium? If you advertise on TV, what types of programs is your target market most likely to watch?

In the last activity, you did what advertisers try to do as they investigate questions like those above. You tried to find out what various people of different ages are watching and what they like and dislike about television.

Television and advertising depend on each other. Television needs advertising in order to make money and thus to survive. Advertising needs television in order to reach the largest number of people. This is where ratings come in.

Ratings are the results of professional surveys that measure how well programs attract audiences in relation to other programs. Measuring people's TV-watching habits is a very sophisticated business. For television, companies such as A.C. Nielsen of Canada Limited and the Bureau of Broadcast Measurement are in the multi-million dollar business of collecting the data that yield such information. Using households that are considered to be representative of all households in Canada, these companies conduct regular surveys of who watches what, when, and for how long. The "who" information includes data on age, gender, occupation, educational background, and geographical location.

The highly accurate results of these surveys are compiled in reports that are made to both TV networks and advertisers. Naturally, the programs that receive the highest ratings, or scores, are the ones on which advertisers will want their commercials to appear, because these shows are obviously reaching the largest audience. The assumption is that the larger the audience, the more product or service that will be sold.

Please be sure to report ALL your viewing . . . including Pay TV and VCR usage.

2

6:00 A.M.

MONDAY

	TIME	TV SET		STATION		NAME OF PROGRAM	1	2	3	4	5	6	7	8	9	Others
	QUARTER-HOURS	OFF	ON	CALL LETTERS	CHAN. NO.	(For Movies, please show Name of Movie.)										
01	6:00- 6:14						MALE HEAD OF HOUSE	FEMALE HEAD OF HOUSE								
02	6:15- 6:29															
03	6:30- 6:44															
04	6:45- 6:59															
05	7:00- 7:14															
06	7:15- 7:29															
07	7:30- 7:44															
08	7:45- 7:59															
09	8:00- 8:14															
10	8:15- 8:29					SAMPLE										
11	8:30- 8:44															
12	8:45- 8:59															
13	9:00- 9:14															
14	9:15- 9:29															
15	9:30- 9:44															
16	9:45- 9:59															
17	10:00-10:14															
18	10:15-10:29															
19	10:30-10:44															
20	10:45-10:59						1	2	3	4	5	6	7	8	9	Other

DAYTIME

	TIME	OFF	ON	CALL LETTERS	CHAN. NO.	NAME OF PROGRAM	1	2	3	4	5	6	7	8	9	Other
21	11:00-11:14															
22	11:15-11:29															
23	11:30-11:44															
24	11:45-11:59															
25	12:00-12:14															
26	12:15-12:29															
27	12:30-12:44															
28	12:45-12:59															
29	1:00- 1:14															
30	1:15- 1:29															
31	1:30- 1:44															
32	1:45- 1:59															
33	2:00- 2:14															
34	2:15- 2:29					SAMPLE										
35	2:30- 2:44															
36	2:45- 2:59															
37	3:00- 3:14															
38	3:15- 3:29															
39	3:30- 3:44															
40	3:45- 3:59						1	2	3	4	5	6	7	8	9	Other

4:00 P.M.

Important . . . Please write in the date you start this Diary ____________________

F·Y·I

Each rating point represents approximately 900 000 households, which in turn are estimated to represent 2.25 million viewers. Based on the value assigned by the rating companies, each percentage point represents millions of dollars in income in commercial advertising per year for a television network. Shows with low ratings (less than 17 in the United States, and less than 2 in Canada) are often cancelled or moved to another time.

For years, "The Cosby Show" consistently received very high television ratings (i.e., over 30). Other types of TV shows that regularly produce high ratings include major sports events; movie, television, and music award shows; royal visits to North America; and interviews with well-known people by outstanding television interviewers.

Television networks use the ratings data to decide which shows will be continued, changed, or cancelled. If it is felt that a change in a show will improve its ratings, sometimes new characters are introduced, original characters are "killed" off, or special guests are brought onto the show. Another method is to have episodes of a situation comedy deal with controversial or highly relevant issues, such as serious illness, death, abortion, drug or alcohol abuse, racism, or divorce.

Switching Channels

1. Of commercials currently running on TV, which comes most readily to mind? Why do you think you remember it so well? Do you love it or hate it? Describe the commercial and explain the reason for your reaction.
2. What effect might ratings have on TV viewers?
3. a) What are some concerns that people might have when ratings are given such a high priority?
   b) How else could programs be rated? What system could be used, and how might it work

Countdown to Air

1. Write down the brand names of as many products as you can that you have recently seen advertised on TV. Try to remember generally the commercial for each product. Did the commercial feature a party? animals doing "cute" things? outstandingly attractive people? a celebrity? Compare your list with those of your classmates. Do certain commercials on your list appear on most other people's lists? If so, why do you suppose this is the case? Could it be because the commercial was memorable, or simply because the product is something you use often? Can you think of any other reasons?
2. Put together your own set of ratings or measurement data based on the class TV-watching log that you compiled in the last section. Survey ten class members, using a pre-set rating system, such as asking each subject to rate a show on a scale of 1 to 10, or whatever method you would prefer. Compiling the class log gave you a general idea of your classmates' preferences, but this rating exercise will indicate just how strong their preferences are. See if you can obtain actual ratings for the programs you measured. How do the numbers compare?
3. How are cars advertised on TV? Do they tend to be advertised more at certain times of the day than at other times? How much are cars used in TV programs generally? What type of effect might the use of cars on TV have on the viewer?

On the Set

1.

   Program makers are supposed to devise and produce shows that will attract mass audiences without unduly offending those audiences or too deeply moving them emotionally. Such ruffling, it is thought, will interfere with their ability to receive, recall and respond to the commercial message.

   – Bob Shanks, ABC vice-president of programming

   How do you feel about the opinion expressed above by Bob Shanks? What points could you make to support his opinion? If you disagree with him, how would you try to bring him around to your point of view?

   Jot down as many points as you can to support your point of view. Order them so that you feel they present your point of view most strongly. Now, find someone in the class who supports the opposite point of view and see if one of you can persuade the other.

   Alternatively, you might want to do this activity in the form of a TV debate. Let several teams of two have an opportunity to debate the issue, while the rest of the class votes after each debate as to which argument was more persuasive.

2. "It's not just during commercial breaks that sponsors are trying to sell." Elaborate on this remark in a brief essay. ■

WE'LL BE RIGHT BACK . . .

Television is considered by some people to be a provider of entertainment and information that is occasionally interrupted by commercials. Others complain that it is a massive selling medium that provides some interesting programming between too many commercials.

It is a fact, however, that no top-rated television programs would be available without commercial

Do you watch the commercials on TV, or do you use the breaks to do other things? Have you ever bought a product because a television commercial aroused your interest? Have you ever decided *not* to buy a product because a commercial annoyed yo

Next time you want a cold drink will it be this one, or would any cold, crisp-tasting soft drink do?

sponsors to pay the immense costs involved in producing such shows. One minute of prime-time television costs roughly $100 000 to produce, so someone has to pay for the "free" entertainment that is beamed into people's homes. Advertisers pay an average of $5000 per second to advertise on U.S. network prime-time (usually 7 p.m. to 11 p.m.) television, so this certainly helps to defray the cost. The return for the advertiser, of course, is that at least some percentage of the viewers will buy the product.

Capturing the audience's attention is the prime objective of all advertising, and television commercials are no exception. Have you ever been entertained by a commercial? Amused? Touched? Excited? Offended? Annoyed? If so, that commercial did its job well. Any reaction — even a negative one — is the advertiser's aim, just as long as the commercial is watched and the product's name remembered. ■

F·Y·I

Prime-time sponsors often pay more than $150 000 for a 30-second commercial aired during top-rated U.S. shows.

What's On?

With so much riding on the number of viewers that a program is able to attract, how do TV networks and stations decide what they'll show and at what time of day they'll show it? The ratings provide the basic clue to what TV audiences want, but launching a new show is always a risk. What was popular last season might bomb this season, and what looks like a loser could be a huge success.

One of the greatest problems for TV programmers is the fact that programs are often made as much as a year before they are to be broadcast, and public tastes can change a lot in the interim. A fact of TV life is that the quality of a show, the type of show it is, and the stature of the star are not at all important if the public prefers some other show for whatever reason.

Unlike the radio, newspaper, and magazine media, TV networks and stations seldom are in the position of being people's "favourites." You might hear someone say that they usually listen to a certain radio station, but you will rarely hear anyone say that of a television network or station. Television program selections are constantly changing, so, when scanning TV listings, viewers choose the type of *program* they want to see at a particular time, no matter what network or

Who would have thought that the comedy program "Roseanne" would be such a mega-hit, when its leading characters were nothing like the slim, professional couples usually seen on television?

station is running it. The decision of what programs to run, therefore, has to be based on factors such as:

- What the competition is doing.
- What the public liked during the past season.
- What new life style trends are emerging (for example, as the number of women entering the work force increased significantly, more TV shows featured working mothers or single women in various types of jobs).
- What the public is currently showing great interest in (for example, at one time, programs with Western themes were predominant, at another, shows with medical themes, and at yet another, programs featuring the police and lawyers).
- What issues are gaining prominence.

In addition, a prime consideration in all marketing endeavours is what age group is currently predominant in the population. Because of the huge increase in the birth rate after World War II, for example, television programmers are having to take into consideration that a great majority of their potential audience is now in an older age group. On the other hand, if statistics indicate that young people are watching more TV than older people are, the programmers must take this into account. Deciding who makes up the largest potential audience — and what is going to appeal to them a year from now — is indeed a risky business.

Keeping up to date with public interest trends is vital for successful TV programming. In the 1960s "Bonanza" was one of the most-watched Westerns of the numerous ones available.

"The Mary Tyler Moore Show" seemed to have something for almost everyone in the 1970s, and "Miami Vice" was the choice of many people in the 1980s.

Programming Strategies

Once a network has identified a program with sure-fire appeal, the next challenge is to try to stop people from switching channels at the end of it. To do this, a network will often schedule similar shows back to back in what is called **blocking**. Another strategy, used to attract at least part of a target audience, is to schedule in the same time slot a program similar to one that a rival network is running. This is called **blunting**.

Bridging, starting a major program earlier than a rival network's major program, is also an effective way to capture an audience that otherwise might have wavered between the two programs.

A riskier but often effective strategy is called **countering,** which occurs when a network runs a vastly different type of program at the same time that a rival network is running a major or highly rated show. Usually the competing program is one that will appeal to one of the major age or interest groups that the network's market research efforts have identified.

These programming strategies are usually brought into play most dramatically during prime time.

Another strategy commonly used is called **pacing** – for example, breaking for a commercial just as something exciting is about to occur or just after someone has said something really thought-provoking. This is done to ensure that viewers will be anxious to see what happens and, therefore, will not switch channels during the commercials. If it is a real cliff-hanger, maybe they will even sit through the commercials!

Timing is Everything

The need to keep viewers interested in a program and to showcase advertisers' products to their maximum benefit requires that certain things must happen at certain times before, during, and after a program. Programs are strictly timed to complement viewer anticipation and "swing." Programs begin with opening pictures and theme music, followed by a segment that is timed according to the type of program. Each type of program observes an identical pattern that is punctuated by commercial breaks. The number of commercials to be shown are specified, based on the length of a program: 6 minutes per half-hour program, and l2 minutes per hour-long program. (Unless a sponsor covers the entire budget for a show, only 4 minutes of advertising per half-hour show are permitted during children's programs.) Sample entries in a TV director's program log are shown in the following box.

Sample Program Log Entries

Schedule Times	Segment Title	Running Time
7:00:20	Opening	00:15
7:00:35	Feature film	10:28
7:11:03	"Ride" campaign PSA	00:10
7:11:13	Car commercial	00:20
7:11:33	Feature film	12:18

PSA = Public Service Announcement

Including the types of elements shown in the box, the total time usually allotted to certain types of programs is as follows:

- Drama and comedy series, game, talk, and variety shows: 30 or 60 minutes
- Documentary, nature, and public affairs programs: 1 hour
- Movies, mini-series: 1-½ or 2 hours

Television viewers seem to prefer shows that provide one or more of the following elements:

- Humour
- Controversy or sensational or scandalous subject matter
- Outrageous or despicable main characters
- Wealth, power, or fame
- Music
- Fashionable wardrobes

Even when all of the required elements seem to be present, the life of a TV show or commercial can be very brief. Due to lack of viewer interest reflected in the ratings, a TV show can be cancelled after just a few episodes, never to be seen again — except maybe to fill in a last-minute blank spot in programming. Commercials sometimes have to be re-shot after only several months on the air because styles, tastes, or circumstances have changed.

Switching Channels

1. Look in your local TV listings and try to identify examples of blocking, blunting, bridging, and countering?

a) During a TV program, note when the commercial breaks take place, and count the number of ads occurring during each break. What do you think the target market is? Do the ads seem appropriate for that market?

b) Choose one ad that appeals to you. Analyse the ad in detail. Does it have a story line? How many times is the product mentioned? How is colour used? How is sound used?

Countdown to Air

1. Over the years, there have been successful TV shows about flying nuns, favourite Martians, talking horses, mothers that are cars, identical cousins, genies, heroic dogs, dolphins with human qualities, ordinary-looking people who are actually witches, and furry creatures from outer space.

   Make a list of possible outlandish ideas for TV shows, explaining the type of audience you think would enjoy each show and the reasons why you think these people would enjoy it.

2. Look at the list of elements of preferred TV shows on page 29. Over a period of a week, watch at least one episode of two different types of shows. At the end of the designated period of time, discuss with the rest of the class the programs that each of you watched:
   - What elements from the list did the programs contain?
   - In what other ways might these programs appeal to viewers?
   - Did you enjoy the programs? Why or why not?
   - Did the programs follow what you have learned about pacing and the placing of commercial breaks? In what way?
3. Using a current television drama or comedy, plot where and when certain things happen in the story. What are the exciting points and the low points in the story? Test your results with someone else's. Select several additional shows to see what patterns or sequences emerge that are common to programs of the same type.
4. Using the data you gathered about the class's favourite programs, select the top ten (or however many you would like to deal with). Divide the class into groups and have each group watch one or more shows. Note the types of jobs done by people on these shows. How do you know what jobs they do? How much of their time is spent actually working? Do you think that watching someone at work on TV gives you an accurate idea of what is involved in various jobs? Why or why not?

On the Set

Choose a short story, a scene from a favourite book, or even a children's story. List the main events in the story. Imagine you are presenting the story as a TV drama. Would you change the order of events in any way? Indicate where you would break for commercials, and write a brief description of what would be happening in your story at the point of the commercial break. ■

THE MANY FACES OF TELEVISION

TV Violence

Crooked police, drug dealers, vicious gang wars, arsonists, serial killers, terrorists, and many other examples of crime and violence have been featured prominently on TV for more than a quarter of a century. Shows that deal with issues and events relating to abuse, assault, torture, kidnapping, and murder regularly manage to win vast television audiences. Why is it that violent characters and violent action have been so popular on TV? What is the real attraction? How do we actually respond when we watch harsh, brutal, excessive or even murderous conduct on television?

The networks not only approve violence on TV, they have been known to request and inspire it. "There is so much violence on television," he said [David Rintels, president of the Writers Guild], "because the networks want it. They want it because they think they can attract viewers by it. It attracts sponsors. Affiliate stations welcome it."

– *Daniel Schorr,* Impact of Mass Media, *p. 137*

Yet many people complain about the amount of violence and unlawfulness depicted on TV – including during some sports events such as hockey games. They feel that, in some instances, such exposure encourages some viewers to commit similar acts. Sometimes programs even provide details of unlawful acts.

F•Y•I

People see more guns used on television than any other single item, including the telephone.

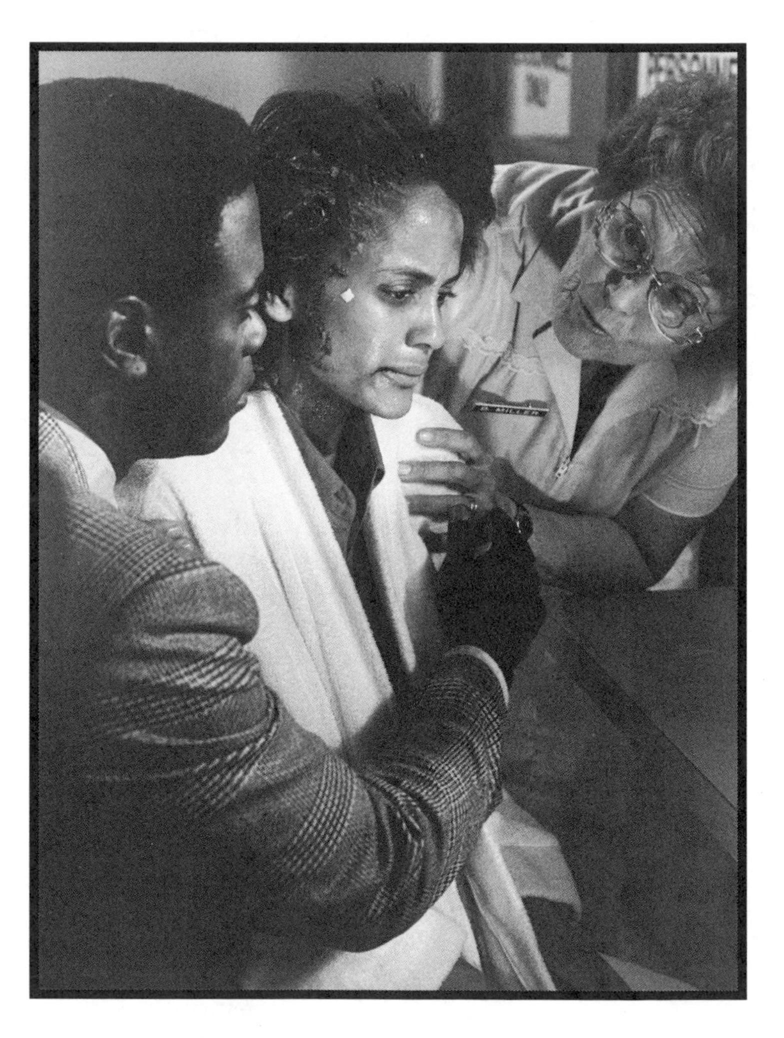

How do you react to scenes such as this when you are watching television?

Food for Thought

Television offers several types of shows that provide learning opportunities in an entertaining manner. Several outstanding nature series, in particular, are available. But the question arises: What exactly do you *learn* from these programs? They are intended as entertainment as well as education. People presenting these programs carefully select the scenes that will be shown so that the viewer won't be bored. Photographers might wait many hours before being able to shoot the scenes they want. Often, creatures are shown doing "cute" things, rather than going about their everyday lives. Is this type of editing really any different from what is done in shows about people? If not, why might it present a problem for the viewer?

Television shows that give viewers food for thought are "Profiles of Nature" (page 33), "Market Place" (page 34), "Science of Architecture," "17 rue Laurier," and "Téléfrançais" (page 35).

Téléfrançais
Leçons
8–11
Téléfrançais
Leçons
5–7

You Are There

With the advent of television, world news took on a whole new meaning. Suddenly you could not only hear the details about a war in another country, an earthquake in California, or the assassination of a well-known political leader: you could *see* the actual event — often very graphically and with several sidebar stories.

It is the immediacy, the feeling of *being there* that makes TV news the preferred medium of information for most people. History-making events stand out far more vividly in the mind when details of the action are seen as well as heard. Few people who watched the first walk on the moon will ever forget it, and the horror felt around the world when the *Columbia* exploded on launching was heightened by the fact that television watchers actually saw the event occur.

Like other programs, news is also entertainment to some extent. Choices have to be made as to the stories that are aired and visuals that are used. In their effort to keep the viewer entertained, those who select stories and visuals for airing have a responsibility to present the information fairly.

Aware that a large segment of their audience is avid to *see* people who would otherwise just be names, television also devotes many hours to coverage of political conventions; elections; addresses by the Queen of England, the Prime Minister, and the President of the United States; state and Royal visits and especially Royal weddings; and charity concerts by famous entertainers.

F·Y·I

A 1986 survey indicated that Canadians spent 33% of their viewing time watching drama-type TV shows and:

19%	News
14.5%	Comedies
8.9%	Variety and game shows
6.5%	Sports

Few people will ever walk on the moon, but many felt as though they were there as they watched the U.S. astronauts' moon walk in 1969. That historic walk was seen by more viewers than any other program before or since.

Kid Stuff

Sit even the liveliest youngster in front of a TV set tuned to almost any program and you've enlisted the aid of probably the world's most-used babysitter. Recognizing this, television provides a wide range of shows with kid-appeal. For many children, the characters on "Sesame Street," "Elephant Show," "Captain Kangaroo," "Babar," and "Mister Rogers' Neighbourhood" are old friends.

Before their first day at kindergarten, many child viewers are familiar with numbers, the alphabet, and the concepts of sharing and co-operating with others. These abilities and values ease their entry into the world of school.

Given these positive considerations, it is easy to overlook a strong negative factor of a large proportion of children's programming: the commercials aimed at impressionable young minds. While most of the above-mentioned children's shows are on commercial-free public television,

"The Elephant Show" and "C'est Chouette," as well as "Polka Dot Door" and "Street Cents" (page 39) are all directed toward younger members of the Canadian viewing audience. "Street Cents" tries to help young people become more knowledgeable consumers.

many other children's programs, especially cartoons, are sponsored by commercial advertisers. Competition for a share of the "youth market" has become compulsory for TV networks and advertisers. They can't afford to ignore for a minute the needs and wants that young people have: toys, food, clothes, hygiene products, sports equipment, hobby supplies, entertainment. They also have tremendous buying power, through their parents.

What this means, then, is that children and young people become targets for TV marketing campaigns. The forces behind these campaigns are well aware of how important it is to reach these potential customers first, before anyone else can sell them products. More and more, TV networks and advertisers are trying to scoop young viewers up when they are still most vulnerable.

Saturday morning television, in particular, bombards children with information about the latest, the best, the most fun, the tastiest, creating a mountain of "wants." In 1980, to protect children from such avalanches of commercials, the province of Quebec banned all advertising aimed at children under 14. Although the law was challenged, it was upheld by the Supreme Court of Canada in 1989.

Statuettes, Sports, and Soaps

Each year, huge television audiences are attracted to shows that celebrate entertainment excellence: the Oscar and Genie Awards for film, the Emmy and Gemini Awards for television, and the Juno and Grammy Awards for music. Fans welcome the chance to root at home for their favourite performers, to see their idols as "real" people, and to admire the stars' extravagant outfits.

Major sports events also draw large numbers of viewers: football's Super Bowl and Grey Cup, baseball's World Series, hockey's Stanley Cup, and tennis's Wimbledon Championships. And, of course, the Olympic Games are covered by all media in the great-

Entertainment award shows and major sports events are never-fail attractions for television audiences.

Continuing a tradition started by radio, television discovered that soap operas were a prime-time gold mine.

est possible detail, no matter where in the world they are held.

A staple of radio programming for many years, soap operas have continued to be a major attraction on television. At first, soaps were scheduled only for daytime showing, attracting a large, loyal audience that waited breathlessly to see if Cynthia would dump that no-good Gregory, or if Trevor would forgive Marcia so that viewers could enjoy a lavish wedding.

Then television decision makers had a brilliant idea: "Since soaps are such good draws in the daytime, let's run some during prime time." And so shows such as "Dallas" and "Dynasty" were hatched — more extravagant in setting and costumes than daytime soaps, featuring better-known actors, and dealing with more scandalous issues, but still the same basic formula. They were hits.

F.Y.I

The term "soap opera" came into use because, in the early days of this type of programming, the product most often advertised was laundry soap. Such shows were run in the daytime only, and advertisers figured that was the best time to reach their target audience with their commercials.

T.V. BREAK

Switching Channels

1. Based on the personal TV log that you prepared in the first section of this book, what percentages of your TV viewing time do you spend watching the different types of programs listed in the "*F.Y.I.*" on page 36?
2. Choose one or more TV programs to watch. Have a partner watch the same ones. Note any examples of violence that you see. Compare notes with your partner. Save your notes for activity 1 a) in "Countdown to Air."
3. Soap opera episodes are among the most widely watched TV programs. What is it about them that appeals to viewers? Would a certain soap appeal to a particular type of viewer or, in your opinion, are all soaps much the same? How do night-time soaps differ from the daytime variety?

Countdown to Air

1. a) As a group, come up with a definition of the word *violence* that would mean the same thing to everyone in a discussion of TV programs. The reason for this is that some people might feel that

a slap in the face is violent, while others would define violence as actual killing of another person.

Once you have a workable definition, discuss the question: Is there too much violence on TV? If the majority of the group feels that this is the case, draw up a list of suggestions that you could present to the government, TV networks and stations, and TV sponsors, as a means of improving the situation.

b) Do you think that the violence that occurs in children's cartoons has a possibly harmful effect? If so, in what ways? If not, how do you think children handle these types of situations?

2. What are the various conflicts that are the focus of TV shows? How do different types of TV use conflict in the same or in different ways?
3. Have you exerted your buying power through your parents recently? How?
4. There are strong arguments in favour of using television in the classroom, and there are equally powerful arguments against using it. Why is opinion so divided about the use of TV in school? Who takes which side in the discussion: parents? teachers? students? business? post-secondary institutions? politicians?

   Prepare a summary of the two opposing positions on using TV in education. Listed below are just some of the factors that have to be dealt with. Remember to cover both practical and emotional impacts.

   - Self-discipline
   - Relationships
   - Attitudes
   - Work
   - Skills
   - Goals

   What would be the most successful way to solve the dispute about TV's role in the education process?
5. In small groups, take a look at sports and news as they are presented on TV. In what way(s) might they be described as "entertainment"?
6. What attracts viewers to game shows? Discuss the importance of the host to a game show's success. If there were no prizes, would people still want to be contestants? Could these shows continue without prizes?
7. Work in a group to compare television news coverage among stations in your area. Have each group member select a channel on which to view a news broadcast in the same time slot over several days. Watch the international news, listing the stories that are aired, the order in which they are presented, the amount of time devoted to each story, and any visuals and/or on-the-scene reporting accompanying the report. (For a more interesting comparison,

select at least one U.S. channel.) Compare your results. Can you draw any conclusions about the way any channel presents its news or about the type of story that it seems to emphasize?

On the Set

1. *Hungry, Thirsty, and Sore: Food, Drink, and Pain on TV* Use words and visuals to present a portrait/collage that illustrates the variety of commercials dealing with these topics.

2. Look again at the videotapes you made for the interview project on page 14. Work with a partner or a small group and select interviewees who have a similar point of view about television. If possible, edit your tape so that only your selected interviewees are seen. If this is not possible, note the counter numbers so that you can fast-forward past interviewees with different opinions. Could you use this material to produce at least two different videotapes that represent differing attitudes toward TV? What might be the reaction of a viewer to either video?
3. a) Develop your own soap opera episode. Write an outline of the plot, give your characters names, and briefly describe the type of personality each character has. Indicate where your commercial breaks will be.
   b) Put together your own consumer affairs program. Do some investigating and testing of various products that are used by people you know—family, friends, other students. Foods, health products, batteries, video games, hair dryers, and chewing gum are a few possibilities. Price, value, quality, and environmental impact might be areas to consider. ■

BEHIND THE SCENES

Producing any television program or commercial is an expensive business. It is not uncommon for production of a potentially top-rated show to cost several million dollars. With so much money at stake, nothing is ever televised until it is certain that the show will be broadcast by somebody who is willing to pay the price for the right to do so.

Three stages are involved in the creation of a television program or commercial:

- **Pre-production:** Raising the money needed for the production; planning (cast, crew, locations, equipment, promotion, organization, legal concerns); preparing the budget for the production; writing the script; targeting the audience and distribution for the commercials.
- **Production:** Staging and shooting of the production.
- **Post-production:** Editing the videotape or film and the sound to achieve the desired theatrical affect.

In Production

Without scores of people working behind the scenes, no TV production would ever make it onto the air. In addition to the key roles played by the people who do the jobs shown in the following chart, vital supporting roles are played by technical directors, camera operators, technicians and engineers of many types, plus multitudes of people with titles that begin with "executive," "co-," "assistant," or "associate." Although each individual is responsible for certain specific tasks, getting any production on the air is definitely a team effort.

Key Television Personnel

Producer	Develops idea for show; works with its creators to come up with workable format, leads, and other "talent." Has complete responsibility for entire project; administers the budget and deals with station management, advertising agencies, financial supporters; responsible for all supervisory personnel working on project and for co-ordinating the technical and non-technical production elements. Often serves as writer in small station operations and sometimes as director of the show also. Sometimes the job of producer is split in two—executive producer and producer—and assistant or associate producers are involved who carry out the instructions of both.
Director	In charge of directing talent and technical facilities; supervises the filming or videotaping of the production in line with the producer's specifications regarding the type of production it is intended to be and the time period it is supposed to represent, while staying within the set budget. Checks blueprints drawn up by set designer; works with set designer to adjust set so that director can obtain certain camera shots and angles. When the show is in production, the director must come up with fair solutions to any problems that arise. The director must always be thinking ahead to what might happen during the show and must be able to recover quickly from any disruption in the show (e.g., a taped report or film clip that fails to materialize during a news show). The director analyses every movement that will take place during the show and decides which camera will catch that movement for the audience. Given that a director of a game show, for example, might have to tape five to ten shows in one day, the director must be a good team leader, capable of defusing stress and obtaining top-quality work from a pressured crew.
Floor Manager (in studio only)	Is the line of communication between the studio talent, the control room, and the audio person; must know where all microphones are positioned at all times and communicate this information to the audio person, who can't always see them; checks that studio lights are working; is the eyes and ears of the control room (where the director and producer are); if necessary, interprets director's information to the talent.
Camera Operator	Follows directions from director; must think ahead to where camera will be next and which kind of movement it will make (forward: "dolly"; sideways: "truck"); must be aware of camera and lighting cables; is responsible for making sure that the camera is operating properly.

Casting Director	Sometimes helps to acquire lead players, but usually is brought in once leads are in place; schedules and runs auditions, call-backs; is familiar with the acting community; "discovers" talent; used in dramatic series or sitcoms, whereas for game shows, a contestant co-ordinator is used.
Production Manager	Usually works closely with the unit manager if the production is big enough to need both; tries to maintain projected budget; works closely with producer and director to juggle available cash, making relevant people aware of costs (e.g., if a special and costly piece of furniture is needed for a set, production manager will discuss with producer and director to decide if that piece of furniture will be used, and, if so, what else can be sacrificed to cover its cost).
Production Secretary	Performs secretarial work relating to the production; ensures that memos are distributed to the appropriate people so that all production crew members are aware of latest developments.
Wardrobe	Plans make-up and wardrobe suitable for type and time period of the production. Wardrobe specialists supervise the design and making of costumes or obtain these from outside sources. Must be aware of fabric designs that cause problems on camera (e.g., designs that show up as a wavy pattern on screen); must choose fabrics that can be used under hot lights (e.g., absorb perspiration without staining).
Make-up	Must be aware of skin types, since make-up that works well for one individual might not work at all for another; takes any allergies into account. Sometimes works in co-operation with lighting director (e.g., make-up and lighting are combined to bring out deep-set eyes). Needs to know how to work with all hair textures. Must be able to provide special effects and latex work (e.g., to simulate scars, burns).
Lighting Director	Must be aware of how different objects on the set absorb and reflect light, how colour works with certain TV cameras. Must know enough about human anatomy to know how to give someone a harder or softer look. Works with set designer and director to understand the mood of the show in order to provide appropriate lighting. Uses techniques to change the texture and quality of light.

Director of Photography	Usually used in commercials but sometimes used in field shoots. Translates the storyboard and the director's requirements in terms of how to accomplish a shot or deal with difficult technical requirements.
Set Designer	Comes up with a set of drawings based on the producer's requirements. Works with the director to adjust the drawings so that the set will meet the director's requirements. Ensures that costumes, furniture, and incidental items such as telephones are suitable for the type and time period of the production. The set designer will often study an actual location (e.g., a courtroom if he or she is designing a set for a courtroom drama). Tries to accommodate the director's shots and come up with ideas to deal with problem or special shots.
Writer	Writes or adapts the original script for TV.
Film/Videotape Editor	Selects the takes of each shot that are best for the production and puts them in the order called for in the script, under the director's supervision. A **take** is a scene filmed or televised at one time without stopping the camera. Often, many takes are necessary before the director feels that at least one take will be suitable. (On a large project, a supervising editor might also be needed.)
Audio Supervisor	Decides on types of microphones and audio recorders to be used and their placement on the set, and controls the audiotaping. Must be familiar with various types of microphones and their capabilities. The audio supervisor is also in charge of the intercom system; is responsible for communication both on and off camera.
Audio Mixer	"Mixes" the sound obtained on the set during the staging of the production to make sure that the sound levels are balanced properly throughout each scene. Adds background music and any necessary extra sound effects. Might add some echo effect or otherwise improve a singer's voice.
VTR Operator	Records items coming in from other sources for news programs; plays them back, as needed, for air. Must be able to solve problems with tapes. Listens to director and script assistant so that needed items will be cued up; must be aware of time, since feed might come in at a certain time on another machine.

Television Assistant	Keeps track of time during live shows (e.g., news); keeps producer informed as to whether program is running too long or too short. Is involved in all aspects of the technical side of TV; assists camera operator, lighting, and audio people; sets up mikes, moves cables, hangs lights; paints flats; sets up and strikes (dismantles) sets.
Editorial Assistant (EA)	Works on all news shows. Does shift work (e.g., overnighting in news room to clear wire copy). Assembles scripts and distributes these to appropriate people. Operates teleprompter so that material can be read by on-camera person who appears to be looking directly at the audience (e.g., anchor reading news). Does filing, photocopying, and faxing.
Talent	Performers, actors, and actresses. Performers play themselves and do not assume the roles of other characters (e.g., talk show hosts); actors and actresses always portray someone else.

Meet a Television Assistant

When Eamon Zekkou graduated from high school in 1978, he was scared. He really didn't know what he wanted to do. Global Television offered him a job, but he chose instead to take a two-year electronics course at community college. He then worked for a while as a video technician, but it was an isolated job that he really didn't enjoy.

After a few months, he accepted the job he had been offered two years earlier at Global — that of part-time television assistant (TVA). Shortly thereafter, he began working on a show with a very small crew. "So I was responsible for everything," laughs Eamon, "looking after the lighting and all the equipment, and making repairs. Since many of these shows were filmed in the United States and Scotland, I even drove the truck and kept track of the crew's expenses!"

He feels that Global's interest in him continued because he did volunteer work, such as helping with telethons, while he was at college. He did so in order to learn what he could about television in a practical way while still at college — and his hard work was appreciated.

When the person in charge of audio left the small crew, Eamon took his place. He has since moved on to become a video operator. In this position, he is responsible for the line-up of cameras and "operational shading" (making sure that all three cameras show colours on the set in the same way and making adjustment if any have too much of one colour).

He expects that his next move will be to the job of technical director, the person in charge of all of the technical aspects of a production. He'll be in charge of the technicians and will be expected to make sure that all of the technical aspects of the production work properly.

Eamon really enjoys his work. The constant contact with people suits him and he appreciates the variety. "There are so many avenues in TV," he says. "It's a fun place to work. I could change my line of work really easily and do something quite different." He stresses the importance of having the right attitude. "You have to have interest, keenness, and background knowledge, and if you're prepared to work hard and keep quiet and learn, you'll make it."

When asked about his ambitions, Eamon said he has no specific career plan in mind: "I just want to be as efficient and happy as possible in any position I hold."

Meet An Editorial Assistant

For Julie Clark, being an editorial assistant (EA) was the first step in fulfilling her ambition to be a television editor. She got the job after working as a part-time summer employee for Global Television.

When she started the job, she had just completed a three-year television broadcasting course at Mohawk College in Hamilton. "You need a community college course in Television Arts or Journalism for this job," explains Julie.

Although it's an entry-level position, the EA's job is demanding because "everybody needs stuff from you for their deadlines." The "stuff" they need is, for example, reporters' scripts. There are seven copies of each script, and these have to be distributed to producers, Chyron operators, production assistants, and others involved in live broadcasts. Each individual has to become familiar with the script in order to time it, adjust its length if necessary, and organize any visuals or other materials that will accompany it. If it arrives late from the EA, everyone's job becomes more stressful. Copy from wire services must also be monitored and delivered to the appropriate individuals.

For Julie, a favourite aspect of being an EA was working on the teleprompter. "It's really hectic because they're always changing the order of items and you have to be on the ball." What she didn't like so much was the shift work. "I work shifts now on my new job, but it's not as bad. The EAs have about ten different shifts, including overnight, and everybody rotates."

After ten months as an EA, Julie became a playback operator. This involves receiving tape feeds from various sources, including requested feeds from affiliates (e.g., coverage of an election taking place in another part of the country). The feeds have to be incorporated into a shot list and assigned to a colour-coded video machine in the control room. The playback operator must know in which order the tapes run and in which pre-assigned colour-coded machine they will go. The job also involves sending out feeds to other stations and pre-recording segments and interviews for shows.

Julie's next step up the ladder was to the job of Chyron operator. "I really enjoyed that a lot," says Julie. "You get to sit in the control room and be part of the whole show." The Chyron is an electronic graphics generator that prints words on screen. When you see a person's name, sports scores, or weather graphics superimposed on the screen, you know that the Chyron operator is at work. Reporters and writers give information to the Chyron operator. If there is time, the operator can key in information and store it according to a list of "supers" and corresponding script page numbers. "It gets complicated." says Julie. "We have a two-channel system, so you can be going to air on one channel and storing material on the other."

Julie is now a videotape editor. "I'd like to stay in this job for a while," she says. "I want to work at becoming a really good editor."

• • • • • • • • • • • • • • •

Before the First Take

All of television starts with a script—the exact words to be spoken and instructions on how they are to be spoken and staged are written in full for entertainment and educational programs, news, weather, sports, cartoons, commercials, and most other types of broadcasts. Basically a script is a manual, a set of instructions, a means whereby a TV program is organized and completed so that people can watch it. The script tries to present pictures and sounds in written language and to communicate a complete idea in sketch or outline form.

Sometimes scripts for dramas and sitcoms are written by freelance writers who then, either personally or through their agents, try to sell the scripts in outline form to a TV network or station. Other times, a network or station will commission the writing of a script by a freelance author (or by a team of authors) or by members of its own writing staff.

Scripts for the various types of TV shows are expected to have certain basic ingredients, as outlined in the following chart.

Basic Ingredients of Various Types of TV Programs

Type of TV Program	Basic Ingredients
Comedy Series	• Certain characters appear in every episode. Each character has a very distinct personality: happy-go-lucky, studious, diplomatic, sarcastic, bumbling, etc. • Humorous predicaments or situations • Situations often exaggerated or highly coincidental • Little conflict • Fast-paced; light; simple • Nothing much changes in the basic series plot
Drama Series	• Same main characters in every episode, plus one or two others • People accomplish something during each episode • Serious predicaments or situations • High conflict; action • Fast-paced; intense; complicated • Each episode has a dynamic climax; things are resolved.
Soap Operas	• Cast of ten or more (much more than in other types of productions) • Interpersonal relationships featured—often stormy • Relationships constantly changing • Characters portray extremes in human behaviour: ruthlessness, greed, unfaithfulness, vulnerability, too-good-to-be-true, etc. • Slow-paced • Each episode ends with a cliff-hanger
News	• Features a news reader (called an **anchor**); often features a co-anchor, usually of the opposite gender • "Specialists" present sports and weather reports • Current arts events sometimes reviewed • Network affiliates can provide international, national coverage; stations prepare local news reports • Some reports enhanced with on-the-spot coverage • Brief, tightly edited news items

Documentary	• Certain subject is reviewed in depth (e.g., prominent people, scientific topic, animal kingdom, history, geography, activities of various types) • Considerable detail provided through interviews, pictures, words, music • Factual; informative • Serious tone
Public Affairs Program	• Host and sometimes guests explore an issue, practice, or phenomenon from the fields of business, politics, education, science and technology, the arts, consumer concerns, etc. • Explores people's opinions, concerns, and experience • Information is shared, conclusions drawn • Fairly factual; usually two or three investigative reporters have been involved in gathering information
Talk Show (classic style)	• Seated host plus guest celebrities, often from entertainment world • Occasional interesting non-celebrities (102-year-old; people with unique hobbies or jobs; award winners in unusual fields; national hog-calling champ) • Mild; jovial, smooth, relaxed, rational • Humour when appropriate • Usually features a house band with a high-profile band leader
Talk Show (new style)	• High audience interaction; host circulates with microphone to obtain audience reaction to guests' opinions. • Focus is on the extreme, abnormal, bizarre aspects of human behaviour • Guests are pseudo-experts, people with experience in the field being discussed, although usually off-beat • Tense, confrontational, unpredictable • Emotional: guests and/or audience members often reduced to tears • Often non-rational.
Game Shows	• Genial, glib host who rarely loses his or her cool • Contestants pre-chosen from written applications sent by people who would like to be on the show, from the studio audience, or as the result of auditions staged for the general public • Questions based on language puzzles or general knowledge in a variety of areas; sometimes contestants have to engage in silly stunts • Fast-paced, but evenly timed • Cash and/or prizes for winners and losers

TV talk shows have been popular on the airwaves for many years.

Certain portions of regular news broadcasts have been expanded to half-hour shows. Global TV's "Sportsline," with its specialist anchors is an example of this new in-depth coverage.

Cut to Commercial

Just as for other types of shows, scripts are required for commercials. The pre-production handling of these is somewhat different from that of scripts for comedies, news shows, dramas,

Sample Commercial Storyboard

For CLOUDLIMIT AIRLINES: 30-second spot

Shot 1:
LS of CLOUDLIMIT jet in blue sky.

Male Voice:
With Cloudlimit, flying is more than it used to be.

Shot 2:
Inside jet now. MS of ATTENDANT giving book to YOUNG BOY. MOTHER looks on.

Music Under:
Symphonic

Music Under:
Continues

Attendant:
I think you'll like this book, Joey.

A storyboard is a panel (or series of panels) on which the required words, sounds, action, and camera cues of a production are laid out, with rough drawings depicting the important changes of scene and action in the production.

etc., however, because an advertiser must be sold on the commercial before it goes into production. As a preliminary, storyboards are produced and shown to the advertiser.

LS = Long shot **MS** = Medium shot **CS** = Close shot

Shot 3:
MS of happy BOY and smiling MOTHER.
Music under: Continues

Mother:
Cloudlimit goes to such trouble!

Shot 4:
TILT UP to CS of ATTENDANT turning to face camera, smiling.

Attendant: Trouble?(beat) *We* (emphasis) call it service!

A Basic TV Script

For most productions other than commercials, the usual first step is a writer's script, which does not contain camera cues and other general staging directions. The writer puts into the script how and what she or he sees and hears happening, to whom, where, when, and maybe why. Beyond that, it is up to the director, director of photography, and the editors to add specific technical instructions.

An excerpt from a writer's script for the weekly series "Degrassi High" is presented on pages 00-00. Note that each actor's job is to make the indicated movements fit with the personalities of the characters portrayed: in a script such as this, the characters might shuffle down the hall, bounce off the walls, be chewing gum or eyeing passing members of the opposite sex, or be walking straight and tall, holding books with obvious care. Whatever the actor chooses to do must be something his or her character would do.

As you read this script, notice what information is given about location, time, characters, their movements, and how that information is presented.

Excerpt from a "Degrassi High" Script (30-minute weekly series)

EVERYBODY WANTS SOMETHING—JUNE 26, 1989

1—INT. CORRIDOR. DAY. **«Day A»**

JOEY, SNAKE and WHEELS come down the hall, toward LUCY at her locker, playing with her video camera. WHEELS carries a handwritten script. In low voices—

WHEELS
I hope she likes this script.

JOEY
Of course she'll like it.

SNAKE
I don't think we should have put in the part about girls hugging us.

JOEY

So? They're not wearing bikinis. And it goes so perfect with the lyrics—Everybody wants something . . .

They arrive at LUCY.

JOEY

(big smile) Hi.

LUCY

(suspicious) What?

JOEY

Remember our video . . .?

LUCY

No.

SNAKE and WHEELS

Come on, Lucy!

LUCY

I said, no. Forget it. Get somebody else to shoot it.

She goes to leave, but JOEY steps in front of her.

JOEY

Wait, wait, wait. We've got a brand new script (WHEELS holds it up). All we ask, is that you read it. If you like it, maybe you'll want to shoot it.

LUCY

. . . You mean, like, I get script approval?

WHEELS, SNAKE and JOEY exchange looks then look at LUCY.

JOEY

Sure, I guess.

LUCY

(thinks, then takes the script) . . . Okay. I'll read it. But I'm not promising anything.

WHEELS, SNAKE and JOEY

(polite) Of course not! No problem. Thanks, Lucy. etc

WHEELS, SNAKE and JOEY watch her go, then eruption —

WHEELS, SNAKE and JOEY

Yes! Alright! etc

GENERIC TITLES

2—EXT. DEGRASSI. DAY. **«Day 1»**

Show titles over kids arriving. JOEY, SNAKE and WHEELS approach. JOEY counts money.

JOEY

We've still got thirty bucks in the budget. Let's spend whatever's left on a party to celebrate when we're finished.

CAITLIN and MAYA have been approaching. CAITLIN lowers her head, tries to pass unnoticed. But JOEY sees her, goes after her.

JOEY

Caitlin, guess what? Lucy's probably gonna shoot our video.

CAITLIN

Great.

JOEY

You wanna be in it? Anything you want!

CAITLIN

I don't think so.

JOEY

. . . You wanna go to a movie this weekend?

CAITLIN

Can't. Sorry.

JOEY watches her go, then starts back toward WHEELS and SNAKE.

JOEY

(shrug) Chicks—who can figure'em?

SNAKE

What's with her?

JOEY

She's moody, that's all.

WHEELS
Moody? She's been like that all term.

JOEY
Everything's fine. And I'd appreciate if you mind your own business.

WHEELS
. . . Sorry.

JOEY realizes he came on too strong. More cockily —

JOEY
Hey, I'm not losing Caitlin. When we finish the video, I'll make everything okay again. Watch — she'll be so impressed by the show, she'll be mine for life.

SNAKE and WHEELS
Right!

The sound of a car horn and they see the Clutchmobile roar up the street.

3 — EXT. PARKING LOT. DAY.

LUCY, ERICA and HEATHER come up the street as the Clutchmobile turns into the parking lot, stops. CLUTCH leans across the seat. Approaching —

ERICA
. . . Poor L.D. How long's she going to be in hospital for?

LUCY
Probably a week.

HEATHER
What do they think's wrong with her?

LUCY
They don't know. That's why they're doing tests. (sees CLUTCH) It's Clutch. Keep walking.

As they speed up —

CLUTCH
(tentative) . . . Hi, Lucy.

LUCY, ERICA and HEATHER start around the car. CLUTCH shifts back over to the driver's window.

18—INT. CORRIDOR. DAY.

ERICA comes around the corner—in time to catch LIZ taping a small poster onto her locker. LIZ turns and sees ERICA. ERICA hurries over and grabs the poster, looks at it. LIZ looks at her defiantly as she reads.

ERICA
(reads) Some toys won't have babies to play with this Christmas.

She looks at LIZ.

ERICA
That's really nice.

ERICA crumples the poster, throws it at LIZ.

ERICA
You did the graffiti, too, didn't you? And the notes. How can you be so horrible?

LIZ
You're the one who's horrible. You're the one who killed a baby.

ERICA
How do you know? And what's it got to do with you?

ERICA shoves LIZ against the wall. LIZ shoves back.

LIZ
Keep your hands off me. I know what you did.

ERICA
You don't know why I did it. Or what it was like.

LIZ
I know you're a murderer.

ERICA
How dare you!!

ERICA grabs LIZ, and they grapple, struggle to the ground—a down-and-dirty, rolling-on-the-ground, hair-pulling, biting fight. They scream at each other. Passing kids don't know what to do, just watch. Finally, MR WALFISH arrives, pulls the two girls apart.

WALFISH

Stop it! Stop it right now!

As he pulls them apart —

ERICA

You bitch! You bitch!

19—INT. CORRIDOR. DAY.

JOEY, WHEELS and SNAKE come out of the stairwell singing away.

JOEY, WHEELS and SNAKE

Everybody get ready/
And get into gear/
The Degrassi sensation/
The one and only/
The Zits are here!

Laughter and high-fives.

JOEY

Man, this is the best day of my life! See you later!

Improvised farewells, and JOEY heads for his class. CAITLIN steps forward.

JOEY

(big smile) Caitlin! Hi! You gonna come watch us make our video? We're doing it today, after school.

CAITLIN

(brittle smile) That's great.

JOEY

. . . What?

She pulls him closer to the wall for privacy.

CAITLIN

We haven't been getting along very well, right?

JOEY

I know, I know. It's all my fault. I've been spending too much time on the video. But that's almost over. After tonight, I'm yours forever.

CAITLIN

. . . Joey, I still like you, but . . . not like before.

JOEY

. . . What do you mean?

CAITLIN

It's nobody's fault. We've gone in different directions. You're interested in your band. I'm interested in politics and the environment. You're fun and outgoing. I'm quiet and boring.

JOEY

. . . So?

CAITLIN

. . . So I think we should stop going out.

JOEY

. . . Is this 'cause of that Claude guy?

CAITLIN

(corrects his pronunciation) Claude.

But she looks away.

JOEY

. . . You're not . . . gonna go out with him?

CAITLIN shrugs — maybe.

JOEY

. . . Oh man.

CAITLIN

I'm sorry. I had to tell you.

JOEY

. . . Okay. No problem. If that's what you want. So, um . . . See you at the movies. Or something . . . I . . . See you.

JOEY hurries away. CAITLIN leans against the wall, feels awful.

20—EXT. SCHOOL. DAY.

JOEY comes out, leans against the wall, shattered, fighting back the tears. After awhile, he starts to walk away from the school. Behind him, the bell rings to signal the start of classes. JOEY keeps going.

21—INT. CORRIDOR. DAY.

The bell rings to signal the end of school. Kids pour out of classes, head home. Announcements over the p.a.

22—EXT. PARKING LOT. DAY.

CLUTCH sits on his car, watches kids pass. WHEELS and SNAKE come out the Southwest door, carrying instruments and a tape deck. Upbeat—

SNAKE
Ta-da! Ladies and gentlemen! The Zits
have arrived! (sound of applause)

WHEELS
Thank you, thank you!

The director takes the writer's version of the script and adds the instructions and details necessary to produce what is called a **shooting script** for the various members of the production crew. The additional information is similar to that shown on the storyboard for a commercial, as illustrated by the sample script for a two-person interview, shown on page 00.

Sample Script for Two-Person Interview

INTERVIEW
DATE: August 6, 19--
PLACE: Studio 1
TIME: 3:00–4:00 p.m.
MODE: Videotape recorder
LENGTH: 10:00 min

VIDEO	
CU of host.	HOST INTRODUCES SHOW.
Host faces camera.	
2-shot of host and guest.	HOST—INTRODUCES GUEST.
CU guest.	
Host turns to guest.	HOST—ASKS FIRST QUESTION.
CU guest.	GUEST ANSWERS.
INTERVIEW: Favour guest with CUs and XCUs.	INTERVIEW WITH GREAT EMPHASIS ON WHAT GUEST HAS TO SAY
CLOSING: 2-shot of host and guest. Host faces camera and closes show.	HOST—MAKES CLOSING REMARKS

2-shot = One of the camera distances between a long shot and a medium shot

CU = Close-up

XCU = Extra-close-up

Less is More

The prime rule for script writing is "less is more"—the more brief, straightforward, and to-the-point a script is, the easier it will be to turn it into a television program. As you can see from the "Degrassi High" excerpt, writing a script is nothing like writing an essay, short story, or book. Scene descriptions are brief and straightforward and each piece of dialogue is short and to the point. Too many words and long, colourful descriptions would make a script cluttered, complicated, and confusing. In television, the camera provides all the extra necessary detail for the viewer, unlike a written work in which the words must provide all of the details.

Furthermore, writing a TV script is never done without everyone involved in the writing knowing exactly who the audience will be. Often the writers have to ask, "What will the viewing public need or expect to see here?" rather than, "What would really happen at this point?" or, "What would I want to see here?"

Finally, writing a script requires the ability to change things repeatedly. A famous TV writer once remarked, "You don't *write* any script for TV; you *rewrite* it!"

Switching Channels

1. What type of job in television could you see yourself doing? What talents or abilities could you bring to such a job?
2. What do you think is meant by the word *conflict* in television terms? Describe some instances of conflict that you have observed in programs you have watched recently.

Countdown to Air

1. Do research on three famous or infamous real people or fictional characters from the past. Then prepare lists of questions that you would ask them if they were your TV guests, and insert their probable answers. Prepare scripts based on the question and answers that contain necessary details for restaging the interviews today: the time period in which the interview would have occurred, the types of clothing that would have been worn then, and the settings in which each interview probably would have taken place. Choose your own characters or select them from the following list.

Cleopatra	Sarah Bernhardt
Hamlet	Sir John A. Macdonald
Florence Nightingale	

Joan of Arc	Nellie McClung
Wright Brothers	Christopher Columbus
King Tutankhamen	Mary Pickford
Calamity Jane	J. Armand Bombardier
Golda Meir	Isadora Duncan
Helen Hogg	Robin Hood
	Alexander Graham Bell
	David Suzuki
	Mickey Mouse

2. **"Breaking down"** a script means dividing areas of responsibility for production purposes. Break down the script sample excerpt from "Degrassi High" that you read earlier. Prepare notes, comments and directions that show the tasks for which people are going to be responsible during production. Assign specific duties to everyone involved. Your goal is a full description and understanding of how the script would be turned into TV.

On the Set

1. Choose a type of product, give it an original name, and prepare a storyboard for the product. Then choose (through auditions) the person or people you want to appear in your commercial, prepare a shooting script, rehearse the script with the talent and the camera operator, and videotape the result.
2. Choose a topic and write a script for a scene or scenes about it, similar to the excerpt from "Degrassi High." Be sure to include details about where the action occurs and when, what is happening in the scene(s) and why, and define the characters and their relationships with each other. If you have difficulty coming up with an idea of your own, you could use one of the following suggestions.
   - Two people are standing beside Niagara Falls at night. A small boat containing two people has been carried perilously close to the falls by the current. It is now wedged against a bush that could give way at any moment.
   - Three or four teenagers sneak into a haunted house. They are astounded by what they find.
3. Make a series of guidance-related videos in which you talk to people in various careers/jobs/occupations having to do with television. Questions you might ask are:
   - What do you do?
   - What do you like and/or dislike about your job?
   - When, where, and how did you get started? ■

QUIET ON THE SET!

In order for a script to be produced, the people concerned have to understand three basic things:

1. Whether the scene is INTERIOR (INT.) or EXTERIOR (EXT.), NIGHT or DAY. Where the scene is taking place (A RESTAURANT, TICKET DESK IN AIRLINE TERMINAL). What actions are being performed by the characters. What sound there will be (dialogue, sound effects).
2. Camera positions (LONG SHOT, MEDIUM SHOT, CLOSE-UP) and camera movements (PAN, DOLLY, ZOOM, TILT).
3. Editing decisions that will be called for (CUT, DISSOLVE, FADE, RESUME, SUPERIMPOSE).

The main idea of a script is to get across what happens, where, when, maybe why, and who or what is involved. Once the script has been finalized to everyone's satisfaction, the cameras are ready to roll.

On Location

At one time, both movie and TV personnel used film to shoot any production. In movie-making, the film was quickly processed so that the aptly named **rushes** could be viewed at the end of each day.

With the advent of videotape, the negative film is processed into a positive videotape. This process is very rapid and the resulting videotape is easier to edit and use, but the process is expensive. All post-production work is now done on tape, rather than on film, and technical advances in this area are occurring constantly. The use of film is usually restricted to shooting dramatic series and for location commercials, because scenes on film have a richer texture and lighting can be used to much better effect. For example, even if filming in daylight, the weather conditions might not be suitable for a particular scene. With the right kind of lighting, film can give the viewer the desired perception. ■

READY FOR BROADCAST

Once a program has been produced, other television networks and stations buy the rights to broadcast it. They then charge local or national advertisers for having their commercials run during the program. Transmitting their signals to their many affiliated stations, networks can assure advertisers of audiences of certain sizes. The greater the number of the potential audience for a program, the higher the price that is charged to the advertiser. If a program does not draw the expected number of viewers, future showings or episodes might have to be cancelled because advertisers will not be interested.

Most private TV stations are affiliated or associated with (not owned by) a major television broadcasting network, because that is the only way in which these stations can make a profit. Since they are unable to pay the kind of money it takes to produce dozens of television shows, these stations broadcast network programs, charging local sponsors for the opportunity of appearing during popular TV shows. Networks like this system because it increases the amount they can charge their sponsors. The more affiliated stations a network has, the more guaranteed viewers it will have.

Technically, the television process is relatively straightforward. Individual stations receive picture signals that the network "feeds" them. They in turn transmit or broadcast the **feed** in their own area.

F·Y·I

Prime-time sponsors in the United States are sometimes charged as much as $150 000 (and sometimes more) for each 30-second commercial aired during hit shows.

The scheduling of a program is also an art, since networks and stations want to ensure that the type of people who will buy the advertisers' products are likely to watch it. So weekday morning schedules are crammed with game and talk shows, afternoons feature soap operas, and evenings are packed with prime-time network comedies, dramas, specials, documentaries, and news programs. Children's programs have their main share of air time before and after school, and on weekend mornings.

When not broadcasting their own or network programs, stations often rerun old movies or old TV shows that are syndicated, which means that the owners of a series sell the rights to run sets of the show's episodes to individual stations.

There also are public broadcasting stations (PBS, often called educational TV) that exist on money contributed by viewers or donated by corporate sponsors, foundations, and government. PBS has a reputation for highbrow entertainment, but in general it just broadcasts programs that would not draw the mass audience required by network TV. TVO in Ontario provides a wide variety of programs in areas such as the arts, children's shows, home study courses, public affairs, science, and youth programming. Again, many of these programs are more specialized than the ones that appeal to a mass audience.

Since 1972, cable television has been a fast-growing phenomenon, particularly in Canada. At present, 7 million of 9 million households have opted for cable company service. These companies pick up signals from networks and stations and then convert them for home reception. They charge subscribers a monthly fee to be hooked-up to their cable viewing service.

Whereas cable television is just beginning in Britain and France, and reaches only 50% of U.S. households, it has developed so much earlier and more fully in Canada because densely populated metropolitan areas close to the U.S. border are able to catch the immensely popular U.S. signals. More remote regions were able to receive cable when, in 1972, microwave dishes and satellites fostered remarkable expansion, even to the high Arctic.

Operating and overhead costs are very low for cable companies because they are not, in effect, broadcasting. They provide a service that processes, boosts, and relays station and network signals to people's homes, enjoying many of the benefits of network affiliation but encountering few of the problems, such as studio costs, need for personnel, pro-

Canada's first satellite, *Alouette 1*, established a longevity record for operation of a complex satellite.

duction, post-production, and advertising. Since the broadcasting apparatus is already in place, cable companies usually set up stations of their own to cover news and sports as well as local, community, and regional affairs.

An offshoot of this is pay TV, for which people pay the cable company monthly fees to receive exclusive network channels that feature sports, movies, news, music, arts, and entertainment.

Since a cable company's range is limited, a number of cable services are always available within a given area. Cable service is relatively inexpensive and usually it is very convenient and efficient. Although cable programming has never been taken too seriously by consumers, there are clear indications that, with some technical improvements and a little more money to produce their efforts, cable TV will enjoy considerable growth and popularity in the coming decades.

Switching Channels

1. Why is it advantageous to networks to have many private station affiliates?
2. What is the service that a cable TV company provides? Why can it provide the service fairly cheaply?

Countdown to Air

If possible, visit a community cable TV station to watch a program in progress. Find out who is involved in putting the program together. What steps are involved? What types of equipment are needed?

On the Set

Prepare a brief program (10–15 min) about events in your school. If you have a school newspaper, you might select your events from it. Give your program as much variety as you can (e.g., use an interview format, an anchor, some group scenes). If you have entertainers in the school, you might persuade one or more to take part. Choose a host for your program and prepare a script. Rehearse each segment of the program and decide how you will move from one segment to another. Use a video camera and practise shooting, trying various camera angles. Incorporate into the script any directions your performers will need.

When you have made your program as professional as you can, make a final videotape and see if your community cable station will run it as part of their community news. If not, make it available for the rest of the school to see. ■

These shows and events provide a pictorial history of some of the programs popular with Canadian viewers since the beginning of Canadian television.

ALLEN

Canada's television industry is very active and produces many programs that are highly regarded in industry circles. The networks that make up the Canadian television system are shown in the following chart.

Canada's Television Networks

Network	Area Served	Ownership
CBC (English)	National	Public
CBC (French)	National	Public
CTV (English)	National	Private
TVA (French)	Most of Quebec and New Brunswick	Private
Global (English)	Southern and eastern Ontario	Private

Most Canadian TV stations buy programming from these networks (as well as from U.S. networks) rebroadcasting them to their local areas. These stations are known as **affiliates.** These affiliates also produce their own programs, such as news, weather, sports reports, and local general interest programs. By having affiliation agreements with national or regional TV networks, however, these stations can afford to show high-budget programs that would be too expensive for them to produce on their own. Such an arrangement also avoids needless duplication of programs — it would not make much sense to have two productions of "thirty something," for example.

Some stations are best known for a particular type of broadcasting. For example, Radio-Québec, TVOntario, ACCESS Alberta, and British Columbia's Knowledge Network offer a wide range of educational programs.

Northern Service Television, established in 1978 in Yellowknife, Northwest Territories, produces its own local-interest programs. It also runs CBC network programs and programs obtained from other sources.

TV and the Law

All television broadcasting in Canada is regulated by the federal Broadcasting Act. The Canadian Radio-television and Telecommunications Commission (CRTC) was established under this Act as an independent authority to regulate and supervise the Canadian broadcasting system. The CRTC regulates both public and private broadcasters and has the power to issue, renew, amend, suspend, or revoke the licence that is necessary for TV broadcasting in Canada. For example, the CRTC has the power to revoke a licence if regulations regarding the numbers of commercials shown per program are ignored.

The purpose of the CRTC is to ensure that radio and TV stations and networks "should be effectively owned and controlled by Canadians so as to safeguard, enrich, and strengthen the cultural, political, social, and economic fabric of Canada." Equally important is that the programming provided should be "of high standard, using predominantly Canadian creative and other resources."

CRTC regulations require that a certain percentage of each day's broadcasting schedule (including during prime time) be Canadian in content, including in key production roles such as writers, producers, actors, composers, and directors.

Some people see this as unfair and unnecessary interference, a form of "reverse censorship" because, rather than being told what they can't show, Canadian television is told what it *has* to show!

What are the results of such strict CRTC regulation? Opinion is quite divided. One side claims that without protection from the CRTC, Canadian television couldn't exist. The other side feels that survival of the fittest should be the guiding law of television. In other words, Canadian networks — including the government-owned and-operated CBC — should have to sink or swim according to their own strengths and abilities.

Of the programs that you watch, either regularly or on occasion, which ones are Canadian productions? Do you feel that these programs live up to the CRTC's goals?

The Beaver vs. the Eagle

Because so much of Canada's population lives close to the U.S. border, most Canadians have had ready access to U.S. television programs since the industry began. Cable TV systems have increased this accessibility.

While CRTC regulations require that a certain percentage of TV programming must be Canadian, all Canadian networks and stations carry U.S. programs; only the commercials are Canadian. The reason is that Canadian networks are in business to make money and Canadian viewers demand many U.S. programs that Canadians simply cannot afford to duplicate.

It is estimated that U.S. programs account for some 64% of audience share for English-language programs. For French-speaking programs, of which 6% originate in Canada, the audience share is somewhat greater. Even in Quebec, however, the size of the audience watching non-Canadian TV programs has been growing.

American TV is killing our culture, students told

WATERLOO (CP)—Canadians are in danger of losing their national identity in a flood of American television images, says the executive producer of CBC's *The Journal*.

"It's possible to show that Donald Duck gets more air time than any French Canadian," Mark Starowicz told journalists from student-run newspapers at a conference this week of the Canadian University Press.

By age 12, the average Canadian will have seen 12,000 hours of TV —10,000 of it American content, he said.

TV stations in Canada air U.S. programs because it's cheaper than producing Canadian shows, Starowicz said. An episode of *Dallas* costs $50,000 to show, but the broadcaster still makes a profit.

"You can't bring in a pig (to Canada) without paying duty, but you can bring in Dallas. Didn't it occur to anyone to say, 'Why don't we tax *Dallas*?' "

Canadians are defining themselves through American TV images, Starowicz added.

For example, there are about 300,000 people in Toronto who are black and whose heritage is the Caribbean, but most Canadians only see TV images of black Americans, he said.

"Our mirror is showing us somebody else's reality."

And with only two full-time TV news correspondents in the United States—the CBC's Joe Schlesinger and CTV's Robert Hurst—there is not much of a Canadian perspective on American reality either, Starowicz said.

As in so many other parts of the entertainment industry, many talented Canadians have gone south to take advantage of the greater potential for work in the larger U.S. movie and television industries. These include such bright lights as actors Michael J. Fox, Margot Kidder, Howie Mandel, Alan Thicke, Donald Sutherland, John Candy, Kate Reid, Leslie Nielsen, Dan Ackroyd, Andrea Martin, writer-comedian Dave Thomas, quiz master Alex Trebek, newsman Peter Jennings, director Norman Jewison, musician/composer Paul Schaffer, and Lorne Michaels.

Vancouver-born Michael J. Fox's success on the U.S. program "Family Ties" led to subsequent starring roles in numerous movies.

Switching Channels

1. What do you think are the differences between Canadian and U.S. TV programs, or do you think they are very similar? Use examples of current television programs to explain your answer. What categories will you use to make your comparisons?
2. When did your local station(s) begin broadcasting? What were some of the earliest programs shown? What were these programs about?

Countdown to Air

1. If the CRTC decided that no U.S. television broadcasting would be allowed on Canadian television, what programs would you watch? Use a TV guide to make up a week-night schedule of the programs you would choose.

   Choose one or two Canadian programs and watch them. If you didn't already know that they were Canadian, could you tell from watching them? If so, how? Identify anything about each show that seems typically Canadian. If the show seems to be simply a copy of a U.S. show, explain why you think so.
2. Read again the newspaper article that appears on page 000. Do you agree or disagree with Mark Starowicz's comments? In 250 words, explain your opinion.

On the Set

Write a scene for a Canadian TV program. You can choose any type of program, but your scene must reflect the Canadian lifestyle, values, or society. Be prepared to offer a brief explanation of what it is about your scene that is typically Canadian and to answer the question: If someone saw your scene as part of a TV program, would they be proud to be Canadian?

THE VIDEO REVOLUTION

As with cable television, the arrival on the scene of the video cassette recorder made a significant contribution to the television watcher's life. Now viewers can watch one program while recording another to view later, or record programs broadcast while they are at work, out for the evening, or fast asleep. In addition, by renting videos of recent hit movies, cultural or sports events, or a multitude of other topics from one of the many video stores now in business, people can relax in their own homes and enjoy the entertainment, without having to pay an admission price for each member of the family.

In addition to those benefits, VCRs and camcorders make it possible for people to create their own TV programs: family picnics and parties, baby's first smile or step, parades, or whatever. Photo albums are being put away, replaced by memories captured in full action and living colour.

Video cassettes are available for many practical purposes also, providing information on a range of educational subjects, home maintenance, health and exercise, hobbies, and business and financial matters, to name but a few. The cassettes are readily available, relatively inexpensive, and, for some subjects, are a more useful way to explore a topic than reading a book.

One controversial aspect of the video revolution, however, is the music or rock video. Directors take a recorded piece of music and come up with images, pictures, and concepts that usually deliver the song in a slick, high-impact visual style. Although many rock videos are not singled out for criticism, overtones and scenes of sex, violence, suggestions of drugs, and excessive stereotyping are found as main ingredients in a significant number of hit videotapes.

Unfortunately some creators get carried away, it's true. They end up putting out videos which are very manipulative. They use the song as a platform and the artists as spokesmen to express messages of their own or the record companies that hire them. That kind of stuff can obviously be dangerous for the teenage audience to see, even if it's only once.

–An award-winning rock-video producer

The Future

Although Russian and U.K. inventors actually led the way by developing devices that would transmit pictures over distances, a U.S. farm boy named Philo Farnsworth was the first person to exhibit public, two-dimensional pictures, an event that took place in Philadelphia, Pennsylvania. In 1938, the United States Patent Office ruled that Farnsworth was the originator of electronic television.

Unfortunately, Farnsworth had to borrow from banks to finance his invention. Eventually, the banks called in the loans and, after years of struggling, Farnsworth faced bankruptcy. So, in 1949, he was forced to sell out to a U.S. corporation, International Telephone and Telegraph, His involvement with television ended soon thereafter, and he died in obscurity in 1971, two years after the history-making television broadcast of the first walk on the moon.

Television has come a long way since Farnsworth's involvement and is sure to experience many more impressive advancements due to advancing technology. Perhaps a glimpse of things to come can be found in Ray Bradbury's novel *Fahrenheit 451.* The story is about a twenty-first century fireman named Guy Montag, but he is no ordinary fireman: his job is to *start* fires, using books and printed material. Books, newspapers, magazines, and other types of publications are banned, along with all other types of media – only television is legal. People have wall-to-wall phono-colour TV screens in their homes, which are called *TV parlours.*

Montag's wife is addicted to her three TV walls. She considers the television characters to be her family, and avidly watches programs of which one part is missing. The following is an excerpt from *Fahrenheit 451.* Also, for one television commentator's view of the immediate future of television, see the article "Future Schlock."

Excerpt from *Fahrenheit 451*

"When it comes time for the missing lines," she tells her husband, "they all look at me out of the three walls and I say the lines. Here, for instance, the man says, 'What do you think of this whole idea, Helen?' And he looks at me sitting here center stage, see? And I say, I say —" She paused and ran her finger under a line on the script. " 'I think that's fine!' And then they go on with the play until he says, 'Do you agree to that, Helen?' and I say, 'I sure do!' Isn't that fun, Guy?"

He stood in the hall, looking at her.

"It's sure fun," she said.

"What's the play about?"

"I just told you. There are these people named Bob and Ruth and Helen."

"Oh."

"It's really fun. It'll be even more fun when we can afford to have the fourth wall installed. How long you figure before we save up and get the fourth wall torn out and a fourth wall-TV put in? It's only two thousand dollars."

"That's one-third of my yearly pay."

"It's only two thousand dollars," she replied. "And I should think you'd consider me sometimes. If we had a fourth wall, why it'd be just like this room wasn't ours at all, but all kinds of exotic people's rooms. We could do without a few things."

"We're already doing without a few things to pay for the third wall. It was put in only two months ago, remember?"

"Is that all it was?" She sat looking at him for a long moment. "Well, good-bye dear."

"Good-bye," he said. He stopped and turned around. "Does it have a happy ending?"

"I haven't read that far."

He walked over, read the last page, nodded, folded the script, and handed it back to her. He walked out of the house into the rain.

Personal (sometimes called **sub-cultural) television** is already growing at a rapid rate. More people want to create their own programming, so new television services are multiplying to meet this demand. Cable companies, for example, are beginning to promote what they call **public access TV**, a form of community service programming on which, for a fee currently ranging from $30 to $150, people can actually go on the air to promote events, make public their feelings about various topics, or demonstrate some talent. Since there are no rules regarding content, some rather unusual home viewing could be the result.

Some observers predict that television will play an increasingly important role in the fields of education, religion, and even criminal rehabilitation. No one expects television to replace schools, churches, or penitentiaries, but its applications could be extended to complement existing services significantly.

As gigantic corporations grow even larger, adding television and telecommunications networks to their lists of holdings, it is inevitable that worldwide TV broadcasting will be developed to transmit to countries such as China, Africa, and India. This will lead to many changes in television programming and production.

Future Schlock

1979–80? Now that was a real fall season. 1999–2000? Well, you can expect 100 channels, a dish on your roof and plenty of reruns on cable

JIM BAWDEN

Ten years ago I sat down at this very desk and tried to write about the 1979–80 fall TV season.

So what's changed in a decade? Well, it's the technology, not the actual shows — they maintain the same standard mix of situation comedies and dramas.

Laptop computer

Ten years later I'm writing this on a laptop computer. My old typewriter has been mothballed. The number of conventional TV channels is pretty much unchanged: CITY-TV was the new kid on the block way back then and Channel 47 was just getting started.

But there were no specialty services, no First Choice, no Sports Network, no Family Channel, no Vision TV. Few people had video cassette recorders and those who did were likely to have Beta machines. There were no Ma and Pa video outlets on every other street corner, offering real alternatives to network TV fare.

So when I'm asked if there'll be a fall TV season in another decade, my answer is a confident ''maybe''.

Is bigger better?

TV screens will get bigger in the next 10 years and the picture and sound will be clearer than ever. But bigger is not better. TV's Golden Age flourished in the '50s, when the networks were trying to entice more people to buy TV sets. When TV hit its saturation point in the early 1960s, the quality went into a tailspin. A captive audience had to settle for lowest common denominator fare.

So 10 years from now there'll be 100 channels. But 100 channels of what? Reruns? More of the same? So far cable has failed to deliver on its promise of rich diversity. So far cable has been snatching away shows we used to watch for free on conventional TV. For the oldest reruns on TV these days, you have to turn to cable.

But TV sets of the future will look and sound much better, that much I can figure out. You know that new set you just bought for your living room? Well, it's already obsolete. HDTV — high definition TV — is just around the corner and will deliver images of pristine clarity. That means it will become ever more expensive to make TV specials and series. But if you want, you'll be able to watch on 100-foot screens — or have a TV projector spreading the image across your largest living room wall.

Cable TV will still be around, but in ever-increasing competition with satellite TV. Perhaps a future prime minister will campaign on the slogan, "A chicken in every pot, a dish on every roof." Satellite dishes will be small and portable and every apartment balcony will have one. Pay TV? I suspect pay-per-view is the future. You'll spot a movie or sports event you want, order it up on your home computer and then it will arrive on special channels with the signal unscrambled.

There'll be more of everything from shopping networks to reruns. Maybe there will even be a nostalgia channel to take us back to the glorious days of 1989.

Bland and unoriginal

Ten years ago, I was previewing such shows as *The Associates; Matt and Jenny; Trapper John, M.D.* and *240-Robert. I thought The Associates* was the funniest new show, but it quickly bombed. I thought *Trapper John* was bland and unoriginal, but it lasted the longest. That's the way TV works: *Trapper John* benefitted from a strong lead-in (*60 Minutes, Archie Bunker*).

And this year? I fearlessly predict *Nutt House* and *Chicken Soup* will take off like *Roseanne* did last season. But I'm secretly hoping there'll be room for *Life Goes On*, too, although I doubt it. TV's lowest common denominator syndrome is still working.

Shady entrepreneurs

And 10 years from now? Will we be watching *Degrassi Senior Citizens* on CBC and seeing the panelists of *Front Page Challenge* wheeled to their positions? Will Mike Wallace still be tackling those shady entrepreneurs every week on *60 Minutes*? Will there be a *Kate And Allie* TV reunion movie? Will westerns be back in fashion? Will *The Young And The Restless* be as young and restless?

These pressing questions I don't care to answer. I'm much too busy worrying about the new 1989 season and wondering which of my favorites will make it. It would be nice to have satellite TV and HDTV and 100 channels to pick from (although *Starweek* would be the size of the telephone directory). But glancing back to 1979 and comparing it with today, I can honestly report that the more TV seems to change, the more it really remains quite the same. ■

F•Y•I

In 1987, there was one TV for every 10 000 people in China. In North America, there were two TVs for each person. Today, there are some 1 billion television sets in use throughout the world.

Some predict there will be major changes in religion and education because of what will happen to TV early in the next century. Now could TV have a real effect in these two areas? It has been said that "seeing is believing." If people see more and more television, and come to rely on it heavily for information, ideas, and values, then what will automatically be the result when it comes to learning and worshipping?

Another view predicts that by 2010 we will have seen everything we could ever hope for on television. We'll be bored, and we'll stop watching the "tube" altogether. They forecast that we'll go back to doing whatever occupied us for thousands of years before TV came along.

These people argue that Western societies will concentrate on traditional things like family and community. Technology will play a much smaller role in our lives. Communication and customs will be simplified and made more personal. Our outlook will switch to reflect a greater concern about clean air and water, and land that we can grow food and animals on. According to this view, TV will become completely outmoded because it will not have any function in our survival.

In the meantime, theatre and film admission prices soar higher and higher. Renting videotapes can often be inconvenient and the selection is not always satisfactory. Less time is available for reading newspapers, books, or magazines. But TV continues to offer ample variety, with no hassles. And the price is a bargain that no other medium can even come close to beating.

Switching Channels

1. How do you react to the quote by the rock video producer on page 86? Give examples from videos you have seen to back up your opinion.
2. a) What type of person is Montag's wife? Do you think it would be fair to say that television has made her the way she is? Why or why not?
   b) What would you guess that Montag read on the last page of his wife's script? Why?

When TV programs are broadcast worldwide, the potential audience for shows will be in excess of 3 or 4 billion people of many cultural and economic backgrounds.

3. What technological advances for TV can you envision? What advances would you like to see occur?

Countdown to Air

1. Set up a TV museum. Use photos, drawings, videotapes, written accounts — whatever appropriate material you can find. Talk to people in your family and within your community who remember the early days of television. Obtain written or taped accounts of their most interesting memories. When your museum is organized to your satisfaction, publicize the hours it will be open, so that others in your school can visit.
2. a) Discuss why "new" is such an important concept for television. Why, in your opinion, does "old" not make for popular TV commercials or programs? What are some exceptions? Why do you think they are exceptions?
   b) TV producers and programmers rely on almost nothing from television's past in putting together current broadcasts. Is there anything to be gained by watching what people used to look at on television? Does it matter that much of TV's programming history is destined never to be known?
3. a) Many books are translated into the TV medium, but the reverse rarely occurs. Why does TV have virtually no place in literary work?
   b) Very few movies have been made about television. "Network," starring Peter Finch and "Being There," starring Peter Sellers, are two of the few examples. Try to obtain a copy of each. What is each movie saying about the effects and impact of television? Which film, in your opinion, presents the most valuable viewpoint?
4. Find out what you can about two-way TV. Is it a reality now or in the foreseeable future? How could it be used in a positive way? in a negative way?
5. One of the wealthiest and one of the poorest people in the world meet and share their impressions of TV. In pairs, take turns playing each role. Summarize the results in a brief report.

On the Set

Prepare a drama based on Philo Farnsworth's life. At what point in his life will you begin? What details will you include? What other characters will be involved?

Prepare a videotape of your drama. Make sure that all pre-production, production, and post-production details are attended to.

Home Box Office: A Simulation

Imagine that you are running a school TV station. You have to obey certain regulations, standards, and rules in your broadcasting effort (e.g., regarding time slots, types of program, etc.). Financially, there is a budget you obtain by selling advertisements to different departments, classes, teams, clubs or groups around the school. Rates of advertising are determined by the audience your station can command.

1. Who is watching your TV station? When?
2. What do they want or expect?
3. How do you accommodate their wishes and so remain in existence?
4. Present a program scheduling profile (guide) for your TV station. Be prepared to justify it in front of:
   a) a group of teachers
   b) a government group that has to check on you
   c) a group of investors
   d) a group of your viewers
5. If possible, produce some of these shows on videotape and broadcast them.
6. Make a point of finding out how your programs were rated.

1 2 3 4 5 4974-6 95 94 93 92 91